ELEGY
for the SOUTHERN
DRAWL

POETRY BY RODNEY JONES

ELEGY

for the SOUTHERN

DRAWL

Rodney Jones

HOUGHTON MIFFLIN COMPANY

BOSTON · NEW YORK ·

For information about permission to reproduce selections
from this book, write to Permissions, Houghton Mifflin Company,
215 Park Avenue South, New York, New York 10003.

Library of Congress Cataloging-in-Publication Data
Jones, Rodney, date.
    Elegy for the southern drawl / Rodney Jones.
        p.   cm.
    ISBN 0-395-95616-1
    1. Young men—Southern States—Poetry. I. Title.
PS3560.05263E44 1999
811'.54—dc21   98-43792 CIP

Printed in the United States of America
QUM 10 9 8 7 6 5 4 3 2

The text of this book is set in Bembo.
Book design by Lisa Diercks

Grateful acknowledgment is made to the following publications, in which these
poems originally appeared:

The Atlantic Monthly: "Plea for Forgiveness," "Raccoon Time." *DoubleTake:* "Ink."
Five Points: "The Assault on the Fields," "Blessed Assurance," "Doing Laundry,"
"Natural Selection," "One Music," "Sacrament for My Penis." *The Georgia Review:*
"Canonical." *The Greensboro Review:* "Crow Time." *The Kenyon Review:* "Elegy for
the Southern Drawl," "Not See Again." *Meridian:* "In Defense of Ugliness,"
"Nihilist Time." *New Orleans Review:* "For Alexis," "In Memory of Al Cohn, the
Humanities Librarian," "The Mind of the Lead Guitarist," "The Perpetual Motion
Machine." *Poetry:* "Central London Time," "Elegy for a Bad Example," "The
Obsolescence of *Thou*," "The Package," "The Poetry Reading," "Refusing to Bap-
tize a Son," "The Secret of William Matthews." *River Styx:* "Aubade," "Holy
Ground." *The Southern Review:* "A Coronary in Liposuction," "The Sorrow
Pageant," "Variation on a Sundial."

for Peter Davison

Contents

We are each of us celebrating some funeral.
   —Charles Baudelaire

The CHANGING
of the PRESENT

For Alexis

I dug a ditch three feet deep and eighteen inches wide
From where the roots had broken through
The Orangeburg pipe and clogged the line

To the end of the drive, and turned and dug
At a perpendicular out a ways and down
To tie in with the junction at the sewer main.

With a shovel and pick, with my sore back
And poet's hands, I accomplished this:
A narrow hole and deep, but undercut at the edges—

The chert kept sliding there. It was like a problem
With law or philosophy. The more
I threw out, the more kept pouring in.

Better the next afternoon when you joined me,
Sweating out your first day home from college
When others might have slept or shopped.

I could not see you, the hole had grown
So vast by then, but heard your rock can
Rattling in the depths, and an occasional

Shit or *goddam,* or an allusion to *The Inferno.*
Did I seem remote? Father was never so proud
Of daughter. We finished excavating by dark,

Snow clouds rolling toward us from the prairie.
That night we were like a Dorothea Lange family,
Hoarding water, using buckets instead of toilets.

Now in late spring I come back to our work,
And the pipe you fitted by cheating at the joints,
Silent in the underground, taking crap, still holding.

Down Time

Where there had been a landscape, I saw everything
Bare and no need for description, now that depression
Had soaked me up: no noise from the pine, the only green.
Sleep bore me on its inward-bearing gale,
Just blood veering off bone, neither voice nor dream,
And when I woke, the weak music of sewage
Rushing behind walls. I needed to lean away
From the face no one would recognize, and the name
No one would call. If I could have imagined
That I was truly alive, I would have wanted to die.
Then, each morning, with a little less dread,
I went out and saw the frost on the lawn
And the awkward water frozen under the bridge;
But for weeks, in the birds limping on oily wings
Across the snow, and the foxes cringing
From dumpsters, I felt my life twinned
With everything that sinks, all the lost women
And men who, finding no door, sleep in the cold,
And the children, beaten down, foundering in disease.
How casually they seemed to bear the knowledge
Of their deaths. And then, poof! It was over.
Light took in the crystals of the thaw. I could
Look into the eyes of others without shame.
It would take time, and still, I was not there,
If there is here, excited again, on the other side.
Before the pleasure of lying with a woman,
There would be the pleasure of washing hands.

Resurrections

Once I was drunk in a foreign city—
I had come to take apart a story,
Downhill from the cathedral,
Through narrow, cobbled streets,
Between walls of bougainvillea,
And turned uphill, and, passing
Under an arch, entered the district
Where the rich people live.
After all, this was a story
Of Ferraris, countesses, and islands,
Not *The Sound and the Fury*.

And this was the next-to-last night
I would get transcendentally smashed,
Break lamps, stain rugs, and black out,
But first I would bestow on the author
Certain invaluable technology
As concerns the workings of plot,
For all you have to do to change
The Man with the Golden Gun
To *Under the Volcano* is reconceive
The descriptions, characters,
And settings, re-register the dialogue,
Parse it, and put it in other mouths.

When I arrived, I wanted to leave,
And when I left, I wanted to arrive.

I remember a vase in the foyer,
African masks on the wall,
The lovely manners of my host,
But not how it got to be light,
Roosters crowing down the block,
A radio crackling—"Jumping the
Reader," Forster called it in his book
On fiction—and is it so bad
To come to, mystically vertical
As though you had entered the story
In the middle, and the police were
Telling it in another language?

My friend Ed, three and a half weeks
After shooting out the lights of the bridge
Between Northport and Tuscaloosa,
Came to in a crack house in the country
In Mississippi. Kids asleep on blankets,
Young girls dancing. Mutterings and ramblings.
Grown-up sorrows. He stumbled out.
Bald dawn. Song over. The naked
Well-digger in the back seat of his car kindly
Directed him to the road to Hattiesburg.

Sometimes in AA I hear those stories,
Just moments really, of abundant
And over-blossoming human time.

How one night, inside the brilliant
Agitation of bubbles in the glass,
The way got lost, and the shame
On the other side of the steadfast
Ambition to feel things deeply
Began to manifest on one shoulder
The magenta tattoo of a cross.
I fidget with my pen and do not speak.

The common account of waking beside
A stranger or coming home to find
The sheets stripped from the bed
And the bank accounts closed
Doesn't mean much, and the things
That get you in court, minor
Embarrassing assaults, insults,
Public urinations, and DUIs,
Are ordinary reasons for speaking up.

How picayunish my drunken strategy,
Perfected years ago in a moment
Of aggravation, to walk the beach
From El Salvador to Los Angeles.
Hard night, we say: hard light
That frames both suicide
And hasty marriage: spin it
A decade or two, it comes back
W. C. Fields or Dean Martin.

The ideal is to speak without
Delusion, expecting no compliment,
Forgiveness being a form of vanity.
After a while you get the feeling
It's not the person weaving between
The lines of self-loathing and self-rapture
But the story that's anonymous.

One boy told of coming to
In a stolen airplane over Kentucky,
Thick clouds, the cops
Two states away talking him down.
Another guy, fat with a florid face,
Told of waking with no ID,
No money, and no idea
How he had gotten from
Minneapolis to Sierra Leone.

I only walked down the hill
And hid while my daughter
Waited for the bus. I asked mercy
At the gate, a little forbearance,
A little silence in the house
While sleep revised me.
I was a tourist in the country of amnesia
Where everyone is Judas facing the Virgin.
Though the prayer there is desperate,
It is offered joyfully, as a child lifts

A bleeding hand to his mother,
And in the manner of the god
Who suffered that we should love him.

The Fruit House

Once I'd let the door bump shut behind me,
The fruit house was a form of suffering.
Its dour lattice of ancient, moldy jars,
Its apparatus of egg sacs and spiders,
Grew suddenly plush as a burial vault.

I wondered, Was the dark invisible?
Did I smell to others as I smelled myself?
What did I really sound like when I sang?
The air held a funk like old, rained-on felt,
Scant oxygen, foot-thick granite walls,

And things I'd put a hand on but no name.
I thought, A few more minutes and mama
Will come with the jars of apple butter;
Then of two men from *Reader's Digest:*
One trapped underwater in a sinking car,

The other waking in a casket, interred alive.
That both survived charmed me a little while.
Not that I'd starve. Not that it was hell—
That would come later when two neighbors
Lowered me through the dark to clean a well.

Owls

Because I had not seen them in the woods until I saw them in a book
And then only a shadow darting among shadows,
I am not going to quote the silence of their wings.

And because before I ever learned the smell of a jonquil
The same essence rose from the chemical
Jonquil in fly poison, I go in confusion,

As one who got the order backwards,
Who learned marriage before sex
And punishment before crime.

A small man, happy with easements,
Preferring the polished image to the dull thing,
I might have sat in the cold moonlight watching.

But the forests were all photographed
And the birds all recorded
When I began. Let the earth separate

My own thoughts from the gray branches of the beech.
After the owls are gone there will
Still be the owl faces in the leaves.

The Pine Forests

Any idiot can see that much of the living green
Has gotten wholly turned into a machine
For our convenience, like a chicken or a cow.
It has gotten put into the packages we unwrap
And the secret decking under our roofs
The way the winter wheat enters a cake,
And it does not care if we chip it in bits
Or ship it to Asia. It does not know
Us any more than it knows itself.
In this paper, beneath these words,
It is not grieving or singing. It is going,
One way or another, to get put back
Into the ground and eaten up. It is all flat
As the soul of my aunt who died as a girl.

The Package

It was a green barn coat from L. L. Bean
That he had ordered, thinking of her
Walking the snowy hillside of his dream
Though she detested the style and color.

That it arrived two days after he died
Did not dispose her to detest it less
Though she may have wished she did,
The way she wished she'd kept house

More neatly or baked instead of fried,
For every coronary's a latent homicide—
If not what we did, what we did not do.
If not what we said, what we did not say.

In this, the inner jury's always out,
No different for man or woman—
For everyone over forty, the human
Condition is grief complicated by guilt.

It's unexceptional really, what's left
After deaths. We're thrown back on our own taste.
That coat, for instance. If that was a gift,
She would have to hide to throw it away.

Variation on a Sundial

The first time I ever got a really good fix on time,
How slowly it moved, how absolutely blunt
And inconsiderate of it not to pass, was in a field,

Nearly lunch. Since dawn, with brutally surgical
Hoes, we had been thinning the young cotton,
And I remember thinking, If I was a boy with a friend

A year older, and he had a friend a year older,
And he had a friend a year older, then we were all
Together in this: the old man Bill, whose father

Had fought at Chickamauga, and the prophet
Ezekiel, and the girl Shirley with snot caramelized
In her nostrils. But in the shade of scuppernong

The sandwiches stayed distant as Nebuchadnezzar.
The rows went ahead and behind and pray, tell me,
What do you plan to do to stop thinking of sleep

When you cannot sleep? On clear days in June
You can make a clock by drawing a circle in the dirt.
If you drive a stick precisely at the origin,

The hour will fall as the shadow of that stick.
You can count the steps to the end of the row. You
Can sing, but the shadow never gets to twelve.

That is the meaning of Zeno's paradox: I would learn
This in the fall of 1970, at the University of Alabama,
In J. D. McMinn's Elements of Western Philosophy,

A semester I wasted, for I would also learn from drugs,
From songs, from the long minutes of short years,
Doing everything three times since I was a Protestant.

I would try very hard to see the present as it changed.
But there where the dark print merged with the dark
And I threw down the book, not marking the place;

There with the tongue which is the prayer of the kiss;
And there above cliffs when I shook my head madly
From side to side and slapped myself to stay awake;

It was not here yet or it was gone. No one told me
I would not know it, for there would not be time,
And from such omissions, the decades would evolve.

Refusing to Baptize a Son

Twilight came and my mother-in-law
Insisting again it would mean nothing,
The ceremony and the holy water,
And happiness of friends and family,
Which is everything to an old woman.
High tide at *el estero,* the Pacific roared

As beer turned to wine and wine to bourbon.
Midnight, fireworks, *Feliz Año Nuevo,*
And us, deep in our cups, and drinking on:
Me with my immutable gringo silence,
And her parrying, "What if he should die?"
And "You don't understand. You're not Roman."

What's changed now that she's buried?
Not nature, not my no, as dumb as yes,
Not the luck of the Spanish armada,
Or high muck I dreamed of defending:
Post-ethnic, post-religious, eclectic—
It's like her heaven. It doesn't exist.

Her spirit does. Stubborn. Procrustean. Loving
The palm tree's lovely freedom from knowledge.
May my son remember his grandmother
Alive in the tropics, standing for him,
Even in these words, even if they mark
The superstitions of an agnostic.

Not See Again

Long I partied hearty with Hogdoo and weird Harold,
One of the hippies waiting the orbit of the strobing joint,
Talking sidemen on the liner notes of albums
And exotic booby traps of Cambodia and Vietnam,
Until, out of money, I compromised and took a job
Working beside Floyd, a pinkish African American
With tattoos up his neck and improbably orange hair.
Meeting, we'd hardly speak, passing the paper slip
We'd consult separately, filling the same order.

Loading boxes on the warehouse's high shelves,
I thought of the sports-car elect, free those afternoons
To motor past the magnolias and daffodils of Greek Row,
And assistant professors cooing toward whispering trysts
In borrowed efficiencies, and desperate women
Shimmying onto the mirrored stage of the Pussycat
To bare and jiggle their breasts for crystal meth.
But also, oddly, each day I grew more attached
To the unspoken etiquettes of that work;

To the secretary Jane, who materialized each morning,
Split skirt flashing from her Triumph's green shine;
And to the men, each with his legend and games.
There was Dalton, infamous for his marriage
To an heiress; and Bayard, who'd served two years
For manslaughter after accidentally shooting
His wife while trying to kill another woman;

And others, remembered faintly from remarks:
"Boss don't fuck with me. He knows I'll cut him."

They called me Buttcut, Shorty, the Presbyterian,
And wanted to know what the notebook was for.
"I'm studying the poetry of Christopher Marlowe,"
I would say, and someone would answer, "Huh"—
Not that *huh* meant anything anyone would want to study.
Even shipping clerks know poetry means romance.
All day Floyd would croon at the top of his bad voice,
The Temptations, Otis Redding, or Stevie Wonder.
And one afternoon he cornered Roy, the foreman,

To say how the night before he'd met a woman
In a bar, and when the bar shut down, they'd gone
To a party way out in the country, a house, music,
Dancing, more drinking, and this is where it got fuzzy.
Either the lights had gone out and there'd been
A fight or there hadn't, but when he came to
The next morning, the car was missing and the girl.
Roy looked at Floyd the way a roofer looks
At sleet. "Goddam," he said, and shook his head.

But the next morning, daybreak, he picked us up,
And we rode around looking for Floyd's car.
Roy drove slowly, grunting as he sucked his pipe.
We circled, hollering to families on porches

Whenever Floyd seemed to remember a bridge or barn.
By eleven o'clock we'd stopped twice for beer.
It hurt Floyd to ask Roy for help, to admit
It wasn't the car, a rusted-out and bunged-up
Oldsmobile, he wanted to find, but the girl.

Roy spoke in an urgently deliberate patois
Of South Carolina, which seemed, in the way
The words got enjambed and the way the vowels
Dragged the voice through the consonants,
To be more singing impediment than speech.
Dalton mumbled of the fifties on the Riviera,
And, as he got drunker, Bayard kept pitching in,
"I told the bitch, come back, your ass is mine."
Okay, it wasn't poetry, but it made Floyd laugh.

We didn't find the car. Christopher Marlowe
Never finished his translation of *Hero and Leander.*
By dark, we'd finished our last six-pack of malt liquor.
The stars had just come out. How lucky I was
To have gone broke, not to have it all regurgitated
For me from a book, but to have lain in a field
With the tongue-tied, the murderous, the illiterate,
And the alcoholic, since I've ended up like this,
The sedative raconteur, the contemplative man.

Central London Time

We made love early and walked by the Thames.
All afternoon we walked, and now,
Caught at closing time between the city
And the underground, we snatched
Our safe house and vantage point

Inside the cordon of a cordoned-off elm
And watched the banking offices void dark-
Suited legions of David Niven men.
Each with his sleek black calfskin
Briefcase and nearly imperceptible

Nod and traffic with the news vendor,
They coursed downhill, broke
Around us, and poured into the tube:
Pinstripes, suspenders, boiled shirts,
And what one naturally makes of power.

Lollygagging at the hard core, dizzy
And aloft on ideas, we were like birds,
I thought, or two Swedish immigrants
In another century and a world away
Waiting inside a train as the buffalo passed.

Holy Ground

One place comes back from my early ranging ground:
A shelf of limestone alive with cedar and cactus,
A sampler of Palestine in North Alabama.
The glinting sewage of blue and brown glass

Made me know that the widow who'd lived below
Had made this unplantable tract a dumping ground.
The rock was pocked and puddled with rainwater
And felt blood-soaked and haunted with prophecy.

What I liked best were the prickles
Of the cactus that bound me to constant
Watchfulness and the whorled grain
Of the cedar branches scattered by the storm.

Stripping the bark, I'd find the balance
Of a handhold, then the stock and bolt.
Others may have seen sticks. I saw guns
To shape and stock carefully among the limbs

Of leafless trees. These would stem invasions,
And if the bomb fell, the one like a club,
Dark red and rich with pith, was the torch
That would lead me to shelter in the cave.

CANONICAL

Crow Time

A summons came from the back of the house,
My mother's voice like a splinter
In my illicit morning with Henry Miller:

The crows were in the pecans behind us.
Already I could hear them squawking
As I made for the closet and shotgun.

By the time I got the shells in the breech,
They'd strung an abacus on a high branch.
And how could I ever kill them?

Before I had the screen door open,
The one perched on the power line,
Whose job it was to watch, had sent them

Off laughing, and no need to follow
Imagery with any generalization
On the fraternity of men and women.

A few things we've hounded from the beginning
Of our time on earth must know us
Better than we know ourselves.

If they vanished in the hickories east,
As I slunk toward them, they would
Circle back low and convene a caucus

Due west in Frankie Appleton's pines.
If I thought as they thought and went
Where I thought they would not be,

They'd flare around me and be gone
With those quick, smirking noises
That seemed to fuse irony to the idiom

Of a discourse sounding something like
"Let's get the hell out of Dodge, boys,"
Or "Shut 'er down, Leon, she's a-pumpin' mud."

Or I could stand there, sputtering like a dud,
While their phenomenon spread
To all things aloof, smart-ass, and hard-to-get,

Or I could go back in and read of breasts.
In those days, I was religion, sprouting myths.
The story would be my own, and not what

Others had said or put in books, but signaled
Straight from the world in flashing codes
Of hurried startings-out and fades to invisibility.

Sometimes the god would be sex, at other
Times death. These were my thoughts
That would not come clear or go away

As I lay in bed, troubling the pages of heaven.
And then, again I heard the racket of crows,
Who were not gods, though surely too,

In all their larceny, loud talk, and glitter–lust,
So much more suitable than eagles
To be ballyhooed as the national birds.

Canonical

My first Chandler & Price letterpress must anchor a tug now.
    Its typefaces have evolved
To the sinkers of a thousand tackle boxes. Its print cabinet
    stands in a cardiologist's breakfast parlor.

It was already an antique when it came to me from the monastery:
    the rollers scabbed with dried ink,
The marble of the compositor's table cracked, the calipers bent,
    the platen warped,

A few woodblocks of praying hands lying around, but only one font
    unblemished and whole.
All the while, in my head, *verily, verily,* and *as it was in the*
    beginning, so . . .

The lightness of my mallet tapping at the galleys of the Beatitudes
    and the Twenty-third Psalm,
Until the phrases went slack, and I claimed the letters one by one—
    That was power.

Then to start afresh, far from the must of tabernacles, the meanings
    blazing in my hands—
I would learn as I worked. You can't just fling them down:
    they're lead

And have to be set slowly, from left to right, with the fine shims,
    the ens and ems
That stand for silence, nothing so filthy as a word.

The Limousine Bringing Isaac Bashevis Singer to Carbondale

A town is the size of a language.

In four more years he would be dead; but now,
A rare hot day in late April,
The middle of St. Louis
And the air conditioner didn't work,
The great black sedan
That Kenny had rented from Mr. D's
Quit, so they had to sit there for more than an hour
Before the tow truck and another car arrived,
Also black, two more hours to Carbondale:
The great man with the great drops
Of sweat registering on his brow.

Perhaps because the faculty
Of every backwater university
Endures by the prescient myth
That even to invite a venerable presence
To read in Starkville or Athens
Inevitably causes grave illness
And to have the person actually show up
Sets the leaves rattling above tombs,
Kenny asked, in that modest
And considerate way he has,
"Have you ever been in a car this long?"

"Oh yes, once in Sweden,
They kept me in a car for weeks."
He got here a little before dark.
He read slowly, deliberately,
A story called "The Missing Line."
When he had finished enunciating
Every word on a page, with a noise
Like a needle ripping the grooves
Of a warped 78, he would ratchet
The page from the staple
And lay it to the side and pause
To take an amplified sip of water

While everyone in the auditorium
Hushed to see if the great old man
Would push through the next hyphen—
Though, of course, the thing was,
The print was small. In the end
He would apologize, though all he did
Was to rush understandably from the elite
Of "The Missing Line" to the pica
Of "The Beard," omitting the last page
Of "The Missing Line." Though
All he did was to pretend to read
What now he began to improvise,
Mating the details of the two stories;
But then, suddenly, knew; was devastated, abashed;

And so had to backtrack and search
Awkwardly before three hundred people
For the missing closure, and so
Would write later, being an honorable
Man, and insist on returning the check.

He was a tiny man with big ears
And palms moist as opened pears.
At the session just after the reading,
When the professors of this and that
Were trotting out those tumors
Of erudition and septic ego
They like to pose as questions,
One of the more sensitive ones asked,
As everyone always asked,
"Why do you write in a dead language?"

And he answered without guile, "Luck."

The next morning one of the students
Asked him what advice he had for young writers.

"I wish someone would write about love."

He had the courage to be simple and precise,
And this would be the last of him.
He would not do it again, no matter the money.

A town is the size of a language.
It is not a language that you would have
Any reason to visit though it is not dead yet.

Nothing survives that has not been scarred
Lovingly in the brain
And dented by the human voice.

The Secret of William Matthews
(1942–1997)

Once he wryly admitted, "I write for friends"—
He was one, but distant—a card from New York
When he bested two dead poets to win a prize,
Shrugging off his laurels, "Stiff competition!"
Though he set those words in a lover's mouth.

Just think of what fun he'd have with these—
"For friends," he said, as though interlopers
Didn't crouch at the margins of those odes
He liked to make to jazz, sex, wine, and food,
Parodying the lucky roll of a shooter's touch.

More likely he was lifting the roof of a house,
To expose not just pleasure but pleasure's
Underside: his natural double-take, one hand
Warning fellow revelers "Don't wake daddy"
While the other cranked up the volume.

Now the body in the work is his, as promised.
There's irony as proof of mythic embarrassment,
And slippery craft and cold technique,
For his music had evolved from the scalier
Anatomies of friendliness and married love.

I see him dapper in sport coat, wreathed in smoke:
One of a generation who refused to grow up,

Or the master addressing his too short letter
(Confidentially and to whom it may concern)
With that blues grace, that singing that talks.

Plea for Forgiveness

The old man William Carlos Williams, who had been famous
   for kindness
And for bringing to our poetry a mannerless speaking,

In the aftermath of a stroke was possessed by guilt
And began to construct for his wife the chronicle

Of his peccadilloes, an unforgivable thing, a mistake
Like all pleas for forgiveness, but he persisted

Blindly, obstinately, each day, as though in the end
It would relieve her to know the particulars

Of affairs she must have guessed and tacitly permitted,
For she encouraged his Sunday drives across the river.

His poems suggest as much; anyone can see it.
The thread, the binding of the voice, is a single hair

Spliced from the different hairs of different lovers,
And it clings to his poems, blond and dark,

Tangled and straight, and runs on beyond the page.
I carry it with me, saying, "I have found it so."

It is a world of human blossoming, after all.
But the old woman, sitting there like rust—

For her there would be no more poems of stolen
Plums, of round and firm trunks of young trees,

Only the candor of the bedpan and fouled sheets,
When there could no longer have been any hope

That he would recover, when the thing she desired
Was not his health so much as his speechlessness.

In Memory of Al Cohn, the Humanities Librarian

How clear it is in Al Cohn's dark blue rage
That he is not here, only December again,
Dark blue, and Al Cohn gone, whose eyes
Were fixed in a thousand books. How clear
That something of Shelley must be saved,
A few of the sonnets like spice for the meat
Of everything that is forgotten, a few
Footnotes of what men did to rescue Herrick
Or Christopher Smart. How clear that
Someone must keep inventory now that TV
And movies obliterate books, and no
One reads the text that is not written,
Which is only the day coming clear beyond
The bare blue spaces among the limbs
Of the oaks in front of the library. The scholars
Wince as they come down the steps,
Polyglots and etymologists, aficionados
Of Berkeley and Raleigh. One squirrel
Greets them, a kind of institutional rat,
Fat and skinny at once, bobtailed, bedraggled
From the first snow. They are not all
Jargon-meisters and gender-benders,
Neologizing, braying the third-hand,
Fourth-rate exegesis. They are not all
Amateur necrophiliacs. And I thought
Of them today because a student wrote
"Swell guys," and another student asked,

"Isn't that wrong, using Old English in a poem?"
How little we have in common, yet the dark
Blue rage of Al Cohn is something, isn't it?
It is his spirit leading the scholars. One has been
Clarifying a misinterpretation of a riddle
Spliced into the second scene of the third act
Of a bad play from the seventeenth century.
One has noted a forgery in *The Book of Common Prayer.*
Some are desperate and many are indolent.
One clutches a Xerox of a washed-out script
That she will spend two summers verifying
As the indisputable handwriting of Samuel Pepys.
For these few perhaps there is no hope.
Stories and poems will always be examples
Of something else, cold and far off, sham
Coins of the primal egotistical wilderness,
Bridges a seminar must cross in its biweekly
Migrations to the country of theory.
It will be five years before they ask, "Where
Is the soul? What is it to be alive?
Which way to the egress?" But for the true
Reader, the one who vanishes into Joyce,
The one who admires Hart Crane only for the sound,
And the one who quit medical school
To spend a year washing dishes and reading Whitman,
If there is a principal angel, it is not tenure,
But Al Cohn's exactness, his rage for humility.

Aubade

What did I say to you to make you rise
Before daylight, dress, and huff off in tears?
What we had was not much—a wooden kiss
Of two bar stools, slow music, that act

So drunken and clumsy, no more charmed
Or perdurable than the chronic masturbation
Of other students, who pieced together
From furtive readings of *Delta of Venus,*

Or interminable, half-slumbering visions
Of classmates in Number Theory or Tagmemic
Analysis, the body of a man or woman—
But it was something. No, I didn't know

Your name either. I knew a story.
One night three aging drunks convinced
A prostitute to take a drive with them
Along the banks of the Tennessee River.

(I heard this on a visit to the circuit court
When I was trying to decide if I wanted to study
Law and end up a powerful, short man,
All day saving the world, and all night making love

To a beautiful woman in a big house
Overlooking a pasture of thoroughbred horses.)

They parked under a bridge and passed around
A pint bottle of Four Roses. Then, slowly,

One at a time, according to the luck of the draw,
The first two fluttered and stalled. But the third
Hovered a long time, slurring his prayer to Eros,
Waiting for his rope to change into a walking stick.

Get off me, you old moron, she told him,
And he did, and still there was the matter
Of the cab fare and the seven dollars.
Fork it over, you old fool, she said,

And he beat her up and left her there,
Naked in the mud. That is why the judge
Had ordered the ladies out of the courtroom.
But you were not mauled or broken, you

With the straw hair and foundling eyes,
Wasting the gift of your extravagant body
To walk at dawn the green headache of remorse.
Of all things, I might have asked your name,

How you lived, where you went in dreams.
I had read many books regarding various
Paths from the breasts down to the thighs.
The sensitive young men of my generation,

Whiling away most of their nights in bars,
Would say it was not their own orgasms
That they enjoyed so much as the pleasure
Of watching the woman get off. They

Would suggest that there were little-known
Areas of the feminine topography,
Passed secretly from bodhisattva to bodhisattva,
Divine chakras along the pale of the foot,

Holy places high on the ball of the hip,
That when touched with a tongue
Or a hand would transport a woman to Nirvana.
But where did you go? Whatever we did,

Two darknesses, so drunken and clumsy,
Twisting the sheets from the bed, making
That full noise—if my joy was your hell,
I hope that is a story you will never tell.

The Poetry Reading

And this is the way it had been done for years in the provinces,
With a nice young assistant decked out in tweed and denim
Standing up at the beginning to evoke some rusty quiddity
Or baroque valentine of the curriculum vitae
To tweak the vanity of the esteemed visitor,
Who would just then be wringing from a backpack
A handful of faded books and the new precious one
That had just from the soul been freshly delivered
And pressed in the black binder, from which
The torqued syllables would soon come springing.

This would be as a wonder to some:
Four who had already heard what was to be spoken
And loved or dismissed it; twelve who had dreamed
Of the ones they had heard of attending,
Who would take off their clothes for anyone;
Five who knew the name but not the work
They had characterized often as promising or derivative;
And two who had blundered into the wrong room,
Thinking to learn of crocodile habitats
Or occult heresies of the Spanish Inquisition.

Still others would be here except that tomorrow
They would be called on to name the elements,
Trample a sonata, or defend a thesis;
If it did not happen on the night of the tournament,
Or on a day when debaters were flapping like puppets
From our greediest and most altruistic intentions;

Or at an hour when Christian bodybuilders
Had donned crucifixes and greased pectorals
To mount scaffolds at the center of the coliseum
And hunch in oddly hopeful positions.

But perhaps the university is not the place for poetry.
Picture our venerable line of shamans, bards,
And nervous wrecks, pulling themselves up
From the sticky kitchens of bohemia
To ascend the rungs of respectability.
Here one drones, whinges, signals with a fist.
Oh it is especially icky when the poet's
Less virile than his photograph, the African's
Too pale, the lesbian is insufficiently militant,
Or the lights make that noise of frying fish.

After all, not much happens in this lounge
Or small auditorium under the library,
And yet those who are here hear, don't they,
Among these lubricated delicacies for the auditory senses,
A thing that is right and singular to the heart?
Oh it does not always have to issue from guilt
Or some lingering inferiority to the British.
It can be done plainly or in elaborate meters.
Afterward, someone still unheard from
May actually go into a room alone and read it.

The Obsolescence of Thou

Last heard in a country church, in a prayer
That an elderly spinster had decked out
In what manner she thought befitting
For heaven's immoderate ears, it seemed
All a Sunday rite and benediction

Except some grave care in its blurting out
Made me think of the papa she'd tended
And kisses forgone for her all-mending,
Hands-on balm and alertness to afflictions
Just surrendered to the cemetery.

But also the way her prayer always ended
("Have thine own sweet way, sweet Lord,
Have thine own sweet way") broadened the context,
So I'd attach it to Pound wooing Keats
("Thine arms are as a young sapling under the bark"),

And love that did get made, often sweetly
(But how soon antiqued and caricatured)—
Not that I'd managed it yet myself,
Just that it seemed prudent to have some sins
To repent, and that one in particular.

ELEGY
for the SOUTHERN
DRAWL

Elegy for the Southern Drawl

1

It is all dying out now in a voice asking,
"Where you from? How ya'll folks doin'?"
On the blank verse of the forklift man,
From way off down there and yonder,
Is draining, thou and thine, from prayers
Of spinsters in the Nazarene Church —
Is dying of knowledge of the world,
But still going, barely, in a grunted "hidey"
In the line at the cash register at Shoney's,
A father telling how he came north
To visit his son, impatience starting up
Its coughs behind him, his *yes'ms* and *no'ms*
An impediment here, Confederate money.
Kid's in my office, slow-talking. I ask,
"Where you from?" He doesn't seem to want
To say, thinks again, then does. "All over."

2

"Local area," my friend Beth Lordan tells me,
Was the code, in the hospital where she worked,
For genitalia, and she would use it
When she was bathing the old and infirm,
From the head down and then from the feet up,
Respecting that one spot, and one day,

Around the waist or the thighs, she stopped
Out of politeness, and asked an old man,
Who was nearly deaf and dying of Hodgkin's disease,
"Do you want to wash your own local area?"
And getting no reply, asked again, louder this time,
"Would you prefer to do your own local area?"
At which he began to nod almost
Ecstatically, saying, "Dublin, Dublin."

3

The old people in the valley where I was born
Still held to the brogue, elisions, and coloratura
Of the Scotch-Irish, and brandished
Like guns the *iffens, you'ns,* and *narys*
That linked by the labyrinthine hollers
Of the foothills of the Appalachian Mountains
The remnants of a people whose dominion
Obtained no less from unerring marksmanship
Than their spiteful resolve never to learn
Any tongue as remote as Greek or Latin,
Much less the Cherokee of Sequoya
That still haunted, like mist, the names of rivers.
"And there was May," my great-grandmother would say,
After May Collum's husband had been cut in half
At the sawmill, "lookin' like the hind wheels of destruction."

4

Country songs, sorghum, the odor of lard
That clung to coats, sweat and saliva roaring
Out of the varnish of old desks as the days
Heated up in late spring: it embarrassed me.
Until fourth grade, I spoke rarely, and then
With a hand cupped over my mouth, I began
To funnel sideways to my friends, as I write
Now in poems, the advantage of poems
In North America being that few will read
Who do not agree that the one in front of us all
Is dotard or tyrant, though at that time,
All the time I was learning the telling of time,
The names of county seats, and division,
I was blotching red with self-loathing,
And mumbling to mask the raw carcass
Of the mispronounced deep within myself,
Which was only the accent of the dying
Language of my South, which is a defeated country.

5

We're riding in the blue Oldsmobile.
Marvin's talking, telling the story

Of the tongue-tied butcher. He's
Working in the back of his shop,

Going with a cleaver at a side of beef
When another tongue-tied guy comes in:

"Cunh me a wump woast when you get tine."
"Fuh wih me you sumbith, I cunya head off."

6

Do you know who this is? the e-mail begins
As it has begun at least four times in the past
Three years, contemporary enigma, without
Accent or signature, only that once
We knew each other, though the language
Is too vague to suggest if we had been colleagues,
Neighbors, or lovers. *Do you know who this is?*
I know what it is to speak without knowing
How it will be received, to take a number,
To sway in a long-decadent tongue as on
A hammock stretched between two pining
Consonants, to audit the gross diphthong,
To pray *Do you know who this is?*, to sound
The vowels where the bodies are buried,
To be nourished by suspense, to emit
Unconsciously the still audioactive rhetoric
Of dead generals, to lie, to know yourself
The instrument and not the song, to wait
For the question *Do you know who this is?*

And not to answer, to become that very one—
Anonymous, everyone's favorite poet
Because there is no profit in it and no ego.

7

When Big Jim Folsom ran for governor of Alabama
A gospel quartet rode in the bus with him, and before
He made the speech he always made,
They would stand on the platform and croon
The song he came to be known for, "Ya'll Come."

He promised to pave the roads, and he did,
And when he ran again, he said, "Before
My first term, I promised to pave the roads,
And I did. This time, I'm holding back one share
For keeping my word," and they elected him, and he did.

He drank, cussed, and philandered. Six foot seven,
Knowing himself, history. And the third time he ran,
A reporter in Birmingham said, "Govunah,
It ha' been repoated that last Sairday night
In Huntsville you slep wi' a nigra womah."

And Big Jim answered, "That's a damn lie,
Manufactured by unscrupulous demagogues
Who have little or no regard for decency,

Mudslingers who wouldn't square the truth
If it up slap and bit 'em. I didn't sleep a wink."

8

I don't know what to say either. Either/either.
"Don't make fun of me. I'm dead."

"You talk differnt. Where you from?"
John Brown asked Gloria—

Five years ago, cloudless Alabama day,
Us returning him to the trailer
From his job mowing the cemetery—

"El Salvador."

"Well, I ain't never been down
There in South Alabama."

9

Some kind of hippie cowboy on the elevator
Going up in the Music City Days Inn,
He's apologizing for his pink hardshell
Guitar case jammed in the closing door,
Thanks, and he's gone, the only white

Man I've heard speaking the hoarse,
Barreled-in English of a native of India.
Later, in the lobby, more cowboys,
Chaws in their mouths like extra molars,
Rhinestone collars, tight black jeans,
Luminous belt buckles, big fellows,
Talking Russian. This is Nashville,
Shrunken world, a hundred twenty miles
North of home. Anna Karenina,
Meet Minnie Pearl. At the bar
Of Tootsie's Orchid Lounge, where
All the rednecks used to dress like Johnny
Cash or Patsy Cline when they came
To be discovered, I stand a welcome toast
To the new line of wannabes: Yoruba
Dolly Partons, Cuban Robert Frosts.

10

Sometimes in one summer, one would hear,
In one family, four or five distinct accents:
Low-country mushmouth; mountain twang;

The almost r-less river talk of merchant planters,
Droned out and of a lazy kinship to the sleek,
Ambidextrous blackspeak of their former slaves;

And the hated northun brogue, smuggled
Back from Dee-troit to parlay credit on a half
Pound of bologna and a box of Velveeta cheese.

Sometimes all of it perched there on one voice,
All the instruments in the symphony
Swaying on the skinny fife of a Scottish reel—

Though the old stuck to their *that theres,*
Their *this hairs, iffens, you'ns,* and *narys*—
Murtis, this hair's my naiphew Graig—

A sentence that, except for the drawled-out
Eccentricities of the rhythms of that place
Between the Sand Mountain Plateau

And the Tennessee River, harbored
Only a hair shallower in the mouth than
The London cockney of a Lebanese immigrant.

11

When the Mongols conquered the Chinese
The males imitated them by wearing their pigtails
And adopting their every custom
Until, after centuries, the Mongols
Who were not married or settled

Lost their place, turned tail,
And fled back into the mountains,
Leaving the pigtail and certain words
That remain chiefly unremarked on,
And persist, like the classic poets
In the south of the North American continent
After two thousand years—just think
Of the ones who answer to Virgil and Homer.

    12

In a recording of Faulkner's speech,
The words wallow and hover: *endyuah*
In a line all to itself, *prevaiah* like Isaiah

Salted and drying behind the tongue—
Just words—no human but the language
Grinding at the shackle of the quotation.

One way to learn a language might be
To forget yourself, ape everything you hear.
Another would be to shut up and listen.

When the line first stretched to our house
And my mother answered the telephone,
I could tell, from her emphasis of consonants

And the tincture and nasality of her vowels,
If she was talking to Grace or Modena,
A habit I hated in her the way I hated

In the exaggerated drawl of country singers
What I took for false emphasis, a pandering
To the cheap seats. Probably,

In retrospect, the way she carried on
With friends rooted closer to the mother tongue,
While the formal, slightly stiff constructions

And Latinate diction she typically used at home
Characterized the language of the country
Where she dreamed my sister and I would live,

Behind white fences, listening to Debussy
And reading Goethe and Shakespeare.
Though also she told the story of an uncle

Who, as a boy, mistook the meaning
Of *sophistication* for *constipation*,
A parable, perhaps, on the fantasy of diction.

She repeated it so often, it began to move
Like a rattletrap with kids hanging from
The windows, and many drivers.

"And how are you constipated ladies
Doin' this morning?" the punch line
Would go, and all of us would laugh.

Particulars, she would say to my sister
When she took a bath. "Don't forget
To bathe your particulars," because

The word *vagina* embarrassed her.
I feel odd hearing a tape of my own voice
That marks wherever I go, the sound

Of lynchings, the letters of misspellings
Crooked and jumbled to dupe the teacher,
Slow ink, slow fluid of my tribe, meaning

What words mean when they are given
From so many voices, I do not know myself
Who is speaking and who is listening.

PIECE
of the WAY

Ink

The enormous new copy station at the center
Of the office, where the assistants gossip
Or sit around joking when they are not
Running off forms and curricula vitae,
Makes me nostalgic for the age of mimeos
And the jelled ink my second-grade teacher,
Mrs. Grimmet, used to make Dittos.
The color of it was like my father's pea coat,
And I would smell it on occasion
Through the seventies, and even as late
As the eighties when I came to work here,
Sometimes I would catch a stray whiff.
It smelled like a book fresh from the printer's.
A few tables remain, the same plastic cabinet,
Burled to ease the transition from wood.
I would come in early to make tests.
The process was boring, methodical,
Wrathful, therapeutic, and cleansing.
In those days, we still used stencils:
Two sheets of paper, attached at the top:
One sheet white on both sides, the other
White on the outside, inked on the inside.
I remember they were called spirit masters,
And as I rolled them onto the platen,
I would feel a nearly metaphysical joy,
As though place were the thing that floats
And atmosphere the prime solidity.
The things we take with us are strange,

And the things we leave behind are familiar.
Coffee brewing, heat whistling in the vents—
Some mornings, after Ben went off his meds,
He would show up dressed in a white
Skirt, light blue blouse, and pearls, and a
Woman who worked here then, the wife
Of a fundamentalist minister, would sob
All the time he talked with Phil, our chair.
Ben wanted an operation, but insurance
Wouldn't pay. "I am a woman trapped
In a man's body," he would say, and then—
As if to mollify the gods of marriage
Or some vestigial heterosexual gene—
"A lesbian." Mostly he was kind, mannerly,
Patient, but soon we began to argue
As to how his appearances should be treated—
Some snickering, others insisting
That the proper response was serious,
Until Charlene, who died recently, said
That he couldn't possibly be serious,
"Wearing white before Easter!" Then,
Of course, he was gone into a hospital.
We had weather to speak of, and happiness,
That pending balance of pain and beauty,
Rose as it rises now, among the dogwoods
And through the ink of papers stacked
On desks where flowers are forbidden
And our work is judged by machines.

Time on the Zipper

On the way to the top, I rode with my son,
And he said, "This is not the way it should be—
I should be the one afraid, and you brave."
"Right," I said, and looked at him, six years old.
The bar on our laps, we rocked in the cage

Across from Wal-Mart and Cinema-8,
And then we jerkingly rose. Just above,
A big kid with a scuzzy beard hollered,
"Top of the world, man, top of the fucking
World!" A hitch there; the clutch engaged:

We dropped straight, the mechanism gagged,
And we were tumbling over and over,
"Like astronauts in training," I told him,
But behind my closed eyes, a guardrail
Flew past and tall ambulances began

Careening toward the emergency room.
A dream, I might have said, but nothing
On earth is ever like a dream until it's over.
Time later to play at son and father—
Now four hands whitened on the rubber bar.

A Puddle for the Theory Group

As I went to check the mail, the brindled–
With-leaves rind of the puddle at the foot
Of the drive was like a chunk of my great-
Aunt's peanut brittle, but when I came back,
It had already oozed into the grass

And was transmogrifying into either
The fault that creeps beneath the entire
Landmass that shifts to hold us, or one
Of those fiddleworms our saws used to sing
Up from the ground to bait a trotline.

I saw this, having just read Merleau-Ponty:
Those dry pages and my catfish river,
Silly visions, but the sun hard at the thaw,
And the wind plating my mustache with crystals.
Clarisse, I thought of you, too: your garlic

Parties, caftans, and crit-lit theories.
But it was so goddam cold. I remembered
Cracking a tooth on that peanut brittle,
And the sound a caught fish made, that singing.
Why can't the river just be the river?

The Mind of the Lead Guitarist

The boy under the tree in Sally Mack Woods is wasting time,
    which is said to pass,
But which seems to him, as the dark gathers, to ooze and trickle,
    with now and then
A squirrel, faintly pattering in the indeterminate distance,
    until there is only
A ticking from far off, like water in a cave. The darkness
    is said to fall,
But he sees how somberly it rises from the fallen leaves.
    He thinks
Of the air inside of rocks, that if he had a guitar, it would be
    a black Flying V or sunburst Les Paul,
That, if this were acid instead of pot, he could hear the wheels
    cracking in the voices of the owls.
He thinks the tree comes up out of the side of the mountain
    like a gang of kids
Running from a night watchman, and one, who wears an old
    pilot's cap,
Says, "Let's split up," which marks the place where
    the branches divide.
It is the place in the lecture where the teacher does not know
    the answer and says,
"There are three aspects of that issue that I would like to discuss." It
    is the place
In "Layla" where Clapton and Allman break into separate melodies,
    a riff at a time,

And farther on, the melodies grow even more various, approach
      manic chaos
For several bars before nodding off and falling again
      into the unifying theme.
The boy has heard that music is not sound but an engraving
      of silence,
That silence is defined by what precedes and follows it,
      and only in this way
Do the moments differ from each other. Meanwhile, choices
      may play some part:
To wear a switchblade earring instead of a cross; to get
      a tattoo of Lenny Bruce;
To change his name to RAM. Tired of being young,
      he despairs of love
And reveres the loneliness of thieves and suicides,
      but the tree is heavy on his back.
He thinks, if the tree were a guitar, it would be a '63 Telecaster,
      and as he walks back
Down the mountain, he plays it, hunching through the trailer court,
      bending the invisible notes.
Let the ones pulling back curtains think what they will.
      It is the beautiful
Tune of his ego that he plays. Neither does it matter that
      they do not hear.
He is already angry at posterity for forgetting his fame.

Raccoon Time

Perhaps in searching for a den, it had squeezed through
The terra-cotta pipe atop the chimney and dropped
In a skittering tumble through the rusted damper
To lie for a while in the soot by the andirons,
Stunned and licking its injuries, and in that instant
Probably did not know itself raccoon, but went on
Out of a habitual raccoon fastidiousness,
Sniffing the ghosts of the chopping block,
Rearing on the piano bench to touch the dry
Black noses of the keys. What did it glean
Of our sealed wilderness and hidden springs?
The faucet dripped. The soap sang in its dish.
We live in a dim inkling or a rapt afterness,
But something was here and one of us for at least
An hour when Gloria shook me from sleep,
Saying, "Quick, the dog has a live
Animal in Samuel's room," and I went naked
And fearless as I was imagining rabbit or bird.
When it wheeled out of the shadow of the bed,
At first it seemed huge as a bear or Bengal tiger,
Making me holler something like huge and rabid
As it went past me in a fierce downgearing waddle,
Spun, and clawed on down the stairs, with first
The dog and then Gloria, beating a plastic
Laundry tub on the rug and going *eee-iii, eee-iii,*
For she is an impetuous woman descended from generals
While I am a person to stand back in emergencies,

Weighing escape routes. I do not ever cross
A bridge but that whole histories of options
Crop up like bubbles from the river's bottom;
As I pulled on my jeans while hearing
The thumps, *eee-iii's,* masked snarls, and shattering
Of pots, the thought of my wife's resolve
So quickly shamed me to the thick of things
That there I was, like a lock on the stairs,
When it found the open door and trickled out,
No Grendel perhaps, though I put it here shining
As if at the center of a heraldic shield,
With her going at it and me standing back
To tell the story. If that is the place of men,
It will be no less glory for me, and she
Will have that image to balance those more
Cautious nights when she defers to my wisdom.

Piece of the Way

When Samuel still could not read
He had ideas bigger than his years
And sometimes as we rode to school
Along McClafferty Road, past

The pond where the deer drink
And the pooled ammonia of pig farms,
He would ask me how high were
The stars, how far did the sky go,

And I would answer as best I could,
Recalling the nights he stood
Cavernous at his black window,
"No one knows how far or high.

Though we know a billion miles
And years, spaces beyond stars,
And dots inside of dots that exist
For the trillionth part of a minute,

Still no one knows, no one gets it,
For as far as we have been able
To see with our best instruments,
There is no top or bottom to it,

And it has no end or beginning.
For always inside the smallness,

There is a smaller smallness,
And always beyond the farness,

A farther farness." "Oh," he
Would say — pleased with himself
For having heard that very thing
And our old truck flying uphill

Past the arboretum — "infinity,"
And hush then, and have no more
To ask that day of any father's
Cosmology, for there are limits.

A Coronary in Liposuction

Hearing how the rope uncoiled from the knot
In John's harness and he fell four hundred feet,
I thought of him at twenty, making poems
Of his work on the high girders, tying steel:

His imagery of cracked welds and icy beams,
And how prone to violence were his men
On probation from jails and stingy marriages.
Before this had sunk in, I had his face

Before me the night I lectured him for slugging
An ex-lover's new friend, and then the body
Going down in the Dragoon Mountains,
Two thousand miles west of Chattanooga,

Where the quintessential grad assistant
Was leading me through the graveyard
Of the new formalists and the language poets
On our way to the fridge for another Heineken;

For this was the festival's first hard-drinking
Wave pounding at the shore of seminars;
Readings and more readings; wine and beer;
And then Gloria calling to say her cousin

Ivey had died of a coronary in liposuction.
I remembered then: nail polish and perfume,

A Salvadoran Liz Taylor, still spiritualist at fifty,
Teetering in spike heels, even at the beach.

She coddled with tantrums and bullied with sweets.
When first we met she'd placed a bet
That she could by her own telepathic wit
Transmit to a distant post a cold Suprema.

For her, I woke early and put one there.
Since then, I've heard from friends
How, at the moment she lay dying in Miami,
A squad of poltergeists stormed the houses

Of San Salvador, toppling statues of the Virgin,
Upending Mayan relics from high shelves;
And also, from Sharon, John's widow, his last
Extruded one and a half words: "Oh fuh . . ."

We were drinking wine late in the afternoon
In a rock garden behind a house in Tucson.
When I told her of Ivey, and got to the phrase
"A coronary in liposuction," she laughed

The great, trembling laugh of beautiful grief.
A horn from the street, and I would be off
To dinner and a reading. West of us the desert
Light grayed indigo, and as it disappeared,

Left the glamour of small, perfect endings.
But my poem does not end there. Not there.
Mid-word in the false altitude of memory.
Not until the knot holds, the surgery takes,

And the fiction of courage and beauty resumes
With the idea that poetry should not flinch:
That they ever lived seems the absurdity.
Not that they died. Until they died, they weren't real.

One Music

On one of those organ chords so flush with notes
    That it brings after thirty years
Not just the salt of dancing clothes
    But the sweetness of a casket's chrysanthemums,

We're floating out on the armory floor,
    Or, spavined from the long train ride,
We're limbering toward the foyer
    Of the colored funeral parlor.

"Midnight Hour" or "Amazing Grace":
    The organist is Miss Viola Wilkins,
Or the band is the Allman Joy.
    We've put a flask of Southern Comfort

On top of a pint of Mad Dog 20/20.
    Or this brother and this sister argue
The spectacles on and off mama's corpse.
    Whoever we are, separate or equal,

Pale trolls or dark angels, we'll grow up
    With these blues in our mouths.
The South won't mourn us. Early
    August, crotch of the year, we're all hot.

Let cities burn. Let Jamesenia Washington
    Brandish her razor at Billy Hopkins.

Let Jeff Davis greet Martin King in heaven.
　　This Otis Redding, Roy Acuff, George

Wallace kind of thing won't go up in smoke
　　Like Detroit or die in Vietnam.
Am I wrong to hear it in the tonic, where
　　All the dissonance resolves?

For five days, while family rolled south,
　　She chilled under crates
Of Nehi cola, packed in the heart of the icehouse,
　　Like an oyster in a box.

The Perpetual Motion Machine

With copper pillaged from busted radios
And shorted-out appliances in the dump,
I would wire the transformer. A generator

Could be bought. I had the motor
Of a defunct washing machine. I had
My inherited blue and red 24-inch

Ladies' Schwinn propped on its handlebars
Between the garage and the pecans.
I had the fire and the book

On Michael Farraday and Guglielmo Marconi.
The way it would work is this:
The front wheel would attach.

To the generator, and when the bike
Began to roll, the front wheel would turn
The generator, which would send

A current swelling through the transformer
Into the motor, which would turn
The back wheel. It would go on and on.

That was the idea. Of my other thoughts
That year, one was of a brain without a body,
That cognition might exist in leaves,

In bits of glass struck by lightning,
That it might occur like my own life,
Secret, dark, incapable of expression.

Another was of bodies without brains,
Real bodies, and so many of just the few:
I do not know where any of them are now.

Nihilist Time

How stark that life of slouchy avoidance,
Thinking all day and all night of nothing,
Alone in my room with Nietzsche and Sartre.
Nothing is what I'd come from, nowhere
Is where I'd been, and I was nothing's man.

Nothing was the matter, I'd not answer
If no one asked, for nothing was the point,
And nothing the view I'd take on faith.
When I died, I'd not be as I had not been
Before I was born, with nothing for a name.

Meanwhile I'd cuddle in a vacuum with my abyss,
Whispering endearing stuff: "My darling
Emptiness, my almost electron, my blank pet."
Later with no one, I'd not celebrate
No event, for nothing was what I loved.

What I hated were people doing things:
Bouncing balls, counting, squirming into jeans
When oblivion waited in every ditch.
I could hear black motors not starting up,
And zeros going nowhere, nothing's gang.

Elegy for a Bad Example

(Everette Maddox, 1944–1989)

If there is no heaven and you are in it,
What does that make me? An idiot?
Your paradise was never the afterlife,
Only the usual after-hours party,
The one with beer and marijuana,

Where the priest, after explaining the rigors
Of extreme unction, happily relieves
Himself on the hostess's potted plant;
Where the engineering student roars
Off naked on the sociologist's Harley;

Where the farm boy turns Buddhist
And the new marriage makes a fist.
Oh but you are not there to quote Berryman,
To enjoin all stupid dreamers to wake up
By the profound example of passing out.

No, in the real heaven that doesn't exist,
You are only the aging of a premonition.
You have no business here. You only occur
To me on a day of many absences
When I give the lecture on attendance.

Advice

If I were you, it would make perfect sense
To listen to what my Aunt Zettie,
In a fit of chuckling, on her ninety-
Eighth birthday, said to my mother
In regard to our Uncle Ollie. Now

He has been dead almost forty years,
But when he was still a young man
And ripping logs into planks at the sawmill,
He forgot himself, his shirt caught,
And the blade severed his left arm
Between the elbow and the shoulder.

Which explains how he came to work
For the railroad, and why I remember him
On a black bicycle, ferrying parcels
Between the post office and the depot.
The only part of the story I did not know
Was that one of the neighbors took
The arm, dressed it in the sleeve of a suit,
And buried it in the Falkville cemetery,

A thing that seemed only reasonable.
But the arm continued to hurt, a phenomenon
Anyone can read of, and that poets love
Because it is called ghost pain, though for Ollie,
The terrible, compelling interest of that pain

Stood like a trestle between him and sleep,
And he had to sleep to work, didn't he?

It makes perfect sense that he would have reason
To listen even to the town crackpot,
A bearded scavenger who interpreted clouds,
Who hung out on the wrought-iron bench
In front of the barbershop and made a spectacle
Of himself, purchasing warts from children.

All the man told him was to dig up the arm
And bury it again, this time not flat like a body,
But vertically, with the hand raised,
The way an arm should be buried
If a man wants to go on with his life.

Maybe it was a dumb idea, but Ollie had it done
And the arm never hurt him again—
What do you want me to say? The oak
Speaks as well as I do. It says, *Listen*.
Whoever you are, if I were you,
I would do exactly what you do.
It makes perfect sense that your pain is not my pain.

The

SORROW

PAGEANT

The Assault on the Fields

It was like snow, if snow could blend with air and hover,
    making, at first,
A rolling boil, mottling the pine thickets behind the fields,
    but then flattening
As it spread above the fenceposts and the whiteface cattle,
    an enormous, luminous tablet,

A shimmering, an efflorescence, through which my father
    rode on his tractor,
Masked like a Martian or a god to create the cloud where
    he kept vanishing;
Though, of course, it was not a cloud or snow, but poison,
    dichlorodiphenyltrichloroethane,

The word like a bramble of black locust on the tongue,
    and, after a while,
It would fill the entire valley, as, one night in spring,
    five years earlier,
A man from Joe Wheeler Electric had touched a switch
    and our houses filled with light.

Already some of the music from the radio went with me
    when the radio was off.
The bass, the kiss of the snare. Some of the thereness
    rubbing off on the hereness.
But home place still meant family. Misfortune was a well
    of yellowish sulfur water.

The Flowerses lived next door. Coyd drove a road grader
    for the county.
Martha baked, sewed, or cleaned, complaining beautifully
    of the dust
Covering her new Formica counters. Martha and Coyd,
    Coyd Jr., Linda, and Jenny.

How were they different from us? They owned
    a television,
Knew by heart each of the couples on Dick Clark's
    American Bandstand.
At dusk Junior, the terrible, would beat on a cracked
    and unfrettable Silvertone guitar

While he pitched from the top of his wayward voice
    one of a dozen songs
He'd written for petulant freshman girls. "Little Patti,"
    "Matilda,"
"Sweet Bonnie G." What did the white dust have to do
    with anything?

For Junior, that year, it was rock 'n' roll; if not rock 'n' roll,
    then abstract expressionism—
One painting comes back. Black frame. Black canvas—
    "I call it *Death,*" he would say,
Then stomp out onto the front lawn to shoot his .22 rifle
    straight into the sky above his head.

Surely if Joel Shapiro's installation of barbed wire and
        crumbled concrete blocks,
In a side room of the most coveted space in Manhattan,
        pays homage
To the most coveted space in Manhattan, then Junior
        Flowers's *Death,*
Hanging on a wall dingy with soot in North Alabama,
        is a comment, too.

Are they the same thing? I do not know that they are not
        the same thing.
And the white dust, so magical, so poisonous: how does it
        differ from snow?
As it thins gradually over many nights, we don't notice
        it; once the golden

Carp have rotted from the surfaces of ponds, there is no
        stench to it;
It is more of an absence of things barely apprehended,
        of flies, of moths;
Until one day the hawks who patrolled the air over
        the chicken coops are gone;

And when a woman, who was a girl then, finds a lump,
        what does it have to do
With the green fields and the white dust boiling
        and hovering?

When I think of the name Jenny Flowers, it is that
     whiteness I think of.

Some bits have fallen to clump against a sheet of tin
     roofing
The tornado left folded in the ditch, and she stoops there
     to gather
A handful of chalk to mark the grounds for hopscotch.

Natural Selection

Hank Nabors was the coach. The team
Clacked out to him. He whistled,
Then began, "Where are you, ladies?"
Blue Devils, dehorned, burned-out, divorced,
Gone to pasture and off your feed,
Backslid and born again, do you remember?

First day of practice in salt-stung, fly-hung
Alabama August's miasma of polleny dust,
We rose up one and took it like men:
The blocking pad, the back scratcher,
The six-mile run, a thousand yards
Of grass drills: the whistle's gears:

First, haul ass; second, retreat; third,
Go lizarding on hands and knees.
Think overdrive. Full speed of music
In your head. Run to beat the band.
Grass drills? The field's bald abrasion mine,
The pysche's mute parental wounds,

And all the girls who thought you odd,
And all the teachers who misunderstood.
I ran for one girl, for Darwin and Freud.
The whistle bleeped. And war came home
Like year-before-last's co-captain
Bagged and buried behind the church,

And what it was to be old, as though underwater
And weighted with lead, you'd half
A mind to struggle as you sank, and so
Stumbled on, or crawled, or cranked
Your old man's body bass-ackwards
As the goal shrank in front of you.

Eight hundred yards, count the dead.
Count gnats knitting sweaters on your teeth,
The breaths from there to here—
Hallucination of defeat: the fatboy bent
In tearful seizure to spritz a breeze
Of Vienna sausage on the field house wall,

The Charles Atlas of our team. And
You, with the birthday wristwatch
Whacking the shank of your bony wrist,
Freshman dickcheese with acetylene
Lungs and a viscous scour of mucus
Drying at the corners of your lips,

Have you learned how Pavarotti
Will sometimes ascend the thick trunk
To that voice trembling at the tip?
What school spirit of the body giving up?
What future in the grass? The beautiful
Human fuel that Whitman saw and is.

Bite your tongue. Think second wind,
Second coming, the cheerleaders
Who'd mate by natural selection with victors:
The unnaturally nimble and nicknamed:
"Dawg," "Big Dooley," "Tore Up."
Sweet Ronnie Duke. "The Duke"

Of Big Dickdom's shower-dallying elite.
Go on. Rehearse revenge, or dream
Yourself the least of the Bear's good
Men, that little thick-necked, quick,
And shoulderless wonder named Stump
Who'd squirt through the Ole Miss line to block a punt.

Band members, do you see us here?—
Our weights and isometrics, our after-
Midnight triple-deckers and gallons
Of milk plaiting a pectoral dream-mail
Like our sisters' puked-out thinness
The mirror refused to show?

Gut-check time, we're wobbling
On three-points. Ten more wind sprints,
We'll race for the right to go in.
I am all right, who did not swing
From an invisible banister on LSD,
Or light hell in the Mekong Delta,

Or quit the team, or knock up anyone.
I ran and saw myself, my place
Outside myself, seventh or eighth,
And studied in each face the physics
And chemistry of exhaustion.
Look again. The ones who come to

The plateau, the wall, the all-I-have
Of not-enough; the hustlers; and
The indomitably gifted look back
And see the town they're from,
And see themselves, a 5-4 team
Grown-up, paired-off, and settled-for.

Or just this one, who represents us all.
The principal now, he still runs
Three times a week, pumps iron,
In late autumn spreads estrogen
On his camouflage and sneaks
To his stand high in a white oak.

And leaves with no deer, no antibody
For his injured senior year. Nights
Watching football on TV, his thrill
Eclipsed, he wallows his middle-age
Couch-cave with the secret ego
Of a martyr who wants to kill.

Sacrament for My Penis

How do I approach it, bald as it is, dangling
Over the urinal to some golden expression
Of lemony bitterness, an old Trappist,
Blind in one eye, kneeling to his paternosters?
Is it mine? It never seemed to be mine.

It was old when I first saw it. A joke
Chaucer might have told but didn't.
A frumpish soldier slumped in a jeep
Above the caption *Dejected Nazi colonel*
Waits to be transported to POW camp.

Yet even now, in the spatulate dark,
Where it lies all day, secret as escape,
Sometimes it will leap of its own volition.
A young terrorist, sprung from prison
And bound for home, bent on sedition.

No, not that—here was my religion—look
Here, blue in the distances of skin—God
Flowers in this nerve. May it remain
Sovereign, inviolable, and unconfessed.
Honor most delicately this feverish guest.

In Defense of Ugliness

As I stand at the mirror before the party,
I imagine I do not see myself, for others
May see me more handsome and dark,
Though the second mirror only adds
The reverse of the same face multiplied.

Well, it is my face; I do not need to look
At it as I drive, but when I am there
In the great room, you come up to me,
One of the gorgeous ones, gone slightly
Fibrous with age, and start to prattle

About the beauty inside as though
You had not married that scratch golfer
Chatting up a sweater across the hall
But his cerebellum and corpus callosum.
"Seeing," you say, "it's all about seeing."

You know what I see. You've read me.
How could I pretend the ugly blessed
Or the beautiful damned, once I had
Learned division? Can't I see you now?
The back of the head is the face of God.

The Sorrow Pageant

High and higher, beyond Guadalajara, the agave queuing up the
    sierra in diagonals strict as tombstones,
The road switchbacking to a narrow pass and threading to the next
    range, a line of trucks ahead
Grinding up into the invisible distance, the Bondoed wrecker in
    front of us, a wreck itself,
Gearing down with such gravity it seemed the whole load of bolts
    and rusty rebar
Would come right back on us, there then. As the gorge thing of
    postcard majesty and grandeur
Wallowed into clouds and reappeared in blowing pockets of clarity,
    we jerked to a stop
And go, stop and go, the minutes stretching out, with now and then
    a man in a cowboy hat leaping out
And stumbling quick to lift a hood and pour water into a boiling
    radiator, before the traffic palsied like a needle
In the hands of an arthritic seamstress. We came bump through a
    tunnel and there it was:
A tractor trailer flipped on its side, and in the grass, blundering
    through the cloud of our bedazzlement,
What seemed at least two hundred hogs: some lamed and hobbling
    in circles; some kneeling
On broken gammons; and others, the gravely wounded, like pillows
    drying on the rocks;
The dead—no one had laughed yet, no one had said a thing, the
    gape like sunlight over everything—
"Because man is no longer a demigod," Joseph Wood Krutch wrote,
    "tragedy, in the classical sense, can no longer be said to exist."

O friends, do you know how the curtain in the brain comes down,
    and the part that will be played
By the public self primps for a moment: the phone on hold, the
    word unsaid? Don't peek there
Where the half-dressed ego counts its aesthetic money: two
    hundred hogs, two hundred Jews
On a train derailed on its way to a concentration camp, what the
    image must mutate to
If it's going to be serious, if it's a scene for the stage, if it's just
    conceptual art, an installation, a dance for radio—
The curtain goes up, two hundred cancan hogs who had gone
    riding piggy-piggy on their way
To becoming the chorizo of Puerto Vallarta. Why did I sit there
    stunned? Poor life, poor stumbling, doddering life!
Broken from its movable zoo and slaughterhouse bondage, so it was
    going to be animation, was it?
One Claymation pig, so luscious and pink, like Kathleen Turner in
    Body Heat, shimmied against our bumper,
And over there, blotto in the shade of a saguaro, W. C. Fields pigs,
    Oliver North pigs.
What had we seen before that the rules of looking depended on?
    Something from the beauty pageant,
Something for the newsroom that came in early on the wires and
    fell behind car bombings and assassinations,
And turned, by midafternoon, to a thing casually remarked on,
    while more glamorous sorrows,
Oil spills and hijackings, kept popping up until who would notice
    it? One of the duds,

One of the sweet odalisques from Omaha who did a campy tap
   dance but filled the swimsuit too full,
One of the Miss Congenialities of sorrow, perhaps to be lifted out
   on a day
When nothing much happened and no one was running for office,
   and held against
The lady who lived to one hundred and eleven by eating nothing
   but fish and never taking baths,
And the extinction of the pine shrew. I wanted the world to see
   those two hundred hogs.
God rest their souls, I wanted to say. God bless their gouged hocks
   and torn trotters. God bless the driver,
Dazed but still alive, standing off to the side with peasants who
   eyed it all, feigning an air of companionable tragedy,
But wondering no doubt if the meat would keep and how to get it
   home to adobe huts where,
Since they had their own TVs, they might learn how today a bus
   full of nuns had tumbled
Down a ravine, or in some far-off and almost unheard-of country,
   another monomaniacal pacifist was deposed.
I hoped they were the kind of men who saw the sweet humor,
   who still believed in fate as perfect expression,
That before they ate, they would give thanks for the phenomenon,
   for the miracle of those pigs.

Blessed Assurance

Never, a brilliant woman told me, trust a man
Who has not been beaten. He will lack compassion.
I wondered, Could that be true? Exactly what
Did *beaten* mean? To look up at a brute
With his arm pinning your neck to the pavement
And plead to be let up, or to have taken
Crap year after year, until the countless small
Arrearages of spite had mounted sufficient gall
To sponsor a shit job that would rent a box
Between a fish market and a muffler shop?

While I chewed this mute host of questions
(what was meant by trust, and what, compassion?),
She drove and talked. I sat and listened,
Just old enough to conjure what had happened
With one man to make her think all men cads
By nature, only weakened to charitable acts
By a father's indifference or a mother's rage.
Did I think, too, of castration? In that age
The word *bitch* came pawing like a raccoon
At the garbage cans of young men's conversations.

And suspicions roared to mark the pratfalls
Of true love a man might suffer, if he lacked balls.
In all of manly silence there's a public caveat—
Not fists or threats, but what manhood's about:
Guard duty in our defeated warrior cult

Made me quiet and made the roadside clutter:
Wrecked cars in yards, chickens on porches,
Barns hardly distinguishable from churches
Where the minister's perpetually in trouble
For laying hands on a dimly languishing cousin.

I still defined *cynic,* all-seeing, half-listening,
Twenty years ago as we rode to a poetry reading:
Our big day's mile-a-minute fields and rivers;
Between us, Diet Pepsi, octane of some wisdom
Of grandma's strained through Simone Weil—
But once I'd heard it clearly, another nail
In the coffin of things I'd secretly expected—
When Alabamians write the text on sexual
Harassment, the title will be *Good Breeding*—
Best concentrate on poems I'd be reading.

Soon we'd reach a city, its theater like a cyst
On the old train station. Did poetry exist
Down there in lingering dreams of horses,
In songs from the radio, and sacred verses
Children recite in vacation Bible school?
Or would our poems strike the vagrant local
Soul like spiced tea and the word *frisson,*
Funded by the Tri-States Arts Commission,
And followed by "I liked the one about the time . . . ,"
"I don't get it," and "Can't you make it rhyme?"

Down-home trust rhymes first with lust. Most
Live in private bewilderment, a kind of mist
Where stories keep bumping into questions:
That and religion's zodiac of generalizations
Comprise hick Zen and show how victims win.
But days don't end. They go on in the ruins
Of what's never trespassed, never spoken:
The good beating's southern as fried chicken.
Family or Christ may hide the chauvinist—
No southerner denies the bigotry of idealists.

Doing Laundry

Here finally I have shriven myself and am saint,
Pouring the detergent just so, collating the whites
With the whites, and the coloreds with the coloreds,

Though I slip in a light green towel with the load
Of whites for Vivian Malone and Medgar Evers,
Though I leave a pale shift among the blue jeans

For criminals and the ones who took small chances.
O brides and grooms, it is not always perfect.
It is not always the folded, foursquare, neat soul

Of sheets pressed and scented for lovemaking,
But also this Friday, stooping in a dark corner
Of the bedroom, harvesting diasporas of socks,

Extracting like splinters the T-shirts from the shirts.
I do not do this with any anger, as the poor chef
May add to a banker's consommé the tail of a rat,

But with the joy of a salesman closing a sweet deal,
I tamp loosely around the shaft of the agitator
And mop the kitchen while it runs the cycles.

Because of my diligence, one woman has time
To teach geography, another to design a hospital.
The organ transplant arrives. The helicopter pilot

Steps down, dressed in an immaculate garment.
She waves to me and smiles as I hoist the great
Moist snake of fabric and heave it into the dryer.

I who popped rivets into the roof of a hangar,
Who herded copper tubes into the furnace,
Who sweated bales of alfalfa into the rafters

High in the barn loft of July, who dug the ditch
For the gas line under the Fourteenth Street overpass
And repaired the fence the new bull had ruined,

Will wash the dishes and scrub the counters
Before unclogging the drain and vacuuming.
When I tied steel on the bridge, I was not so holy

As now, taking the hot sheets from the dryer,
Thinking of the song I will make in praise of women,
But also of ordinary men, doing laundry.